THIS TRAINING MANUAL SHOULD BE USED ONLY AS A GUIDE.

No part of this book can be reproduced or transmitted in any form or by any means, Electronic or mechanical, including photocopying, recording, or by any information Storage and retrieval system, without permission in writing from the author.

Writing Effective Incident Reports

Writing reports that are accurate and professional

Introduction

Reports serve as a permanent record of incidents, events, problems, and so forth. There are many types of reports, each of which serves different functions. Some are used to keep people informed of activities within the department. Some are used to compile statistical information, identify problems in the community, or identify department training needs. Some reports are needed to facilitate investigations, prepare court cases, or defend cases in court.

It is beyond the scope of this book to elaborate on the different types of reports used in the emergency response field or on the report-writing process itself. That information needs to come from your particular agency. However, I want to briefly touch on the importance of well-written reports and the characteristics of a good report.

The Importance of Well-Written Reports

Poorly written reports hurt your credibility by making you appear less competent and professional. They can also undermine your goals in a number of ways. A poorly written report can cause you to lose a case in court, perhaps resulting in a criminal being set free to kill, rape, steal, or commit arson again. Poorly written reports can make it difficult to accurately identify training and equipment needs. They can result in failure to take appropriate follow-up action on a problem. And those are just a few examples.

Just as important as content are grammar, punctuation, spelling, and word choice. Something as simple as improperly using or omitting a comma can change the meaning of a sentence. So can the use of a wrong word. It's not uncommon in a court of law for attorneys to attack the credibility of a witness by displaying a report on screen for all to see and pointing out all the errors in grammar, spelling, and so forth. The strategy is to cast doubt on the witness's competency and professionalism. "If the witness is this careless in writing his report, how can we trust that he was accurate, thorough, and attentive to detail when conducting his investigation?"

Your reports can also have unintended consequences for the public we serve. Consider a workplace injury where firefighters or paramedics incorrectly document information given to them by the patient. Consequently, Workers' Compensation denies the patient's claim because of the way something was written in the patient contact report. Fighting to get those benefits restored will be a nightmare for the patient, all because someone failed to be clear, accurate, or specific in a report.

Well-written reports require some effort. They should not be something you merely throw together between calls. You should carefully review and edit each report before filing it or forwarding it to your supervisor. Consider reviewing the report with your crew before submitting it. Make sure it accurately reflects what each member of the crew did.

Good and Bad Characteristics

Common Problems with Incident Reports

The following are common problems found in incident reports:

- Confusing to someone who wasn't there (report doesn't paint a clear picture)
- Thoughts not presented in an organized manner
- Not enough detail (who, what, when, where, why, and how) • Not clear and concise
- Poor grammar, punctuation, and spelling • Incorrect word usage
- Use of terms, abbreviations, and acronyms that readers may not be familiar with
- Inconsistency in style throughout the department

Characteristics of a Good Report

The following are characteristics of a good report (or any other document, for that matter):

- Accurate and specific
- Factual
- Objective • Clear
- Complete
  Concise
- Well-organized
- Grammatically correct
  Light on abbreviations

We'll address each of these characteristics in more detail.

A Good Report Is Accurate and Specific

Emergency responders do not have much room for error in the field. The mistakes we make can mean the difference between life and death for the citizens we serve, as well as for ourselves and our coworkers.

Reports are a little different. You can type the wrong number when documenting a drug dosage, for example, without killing your patient. But the error can come back to haunt you later when your supervisor, the patient's family, or an attorney wants to know why you administered the wrong dosage. Some errors are not discovered until years later when a case goes to court. By that time, you may have forgotten the details of the case. Even if you do remember the correct information, your credibility will suffer when you have to admit you made a mistake in your report. It raises questions about how many other errors you made.

Many inaccuracies are due to simple spelling errors and typos. Spell-check your reports. Double-check dates, times, names, phone numbers, etc. Proof your documents carefully, and have others proof your documents as appropriate. It's often a good idea to set a document aside for a day or two, if you have that flexibility, then proof it again. Often you will see problems you missed before.

Being accurate also means being specific. Vague reference do not give readers much information. The following is an example:

Vague: The accused did damage.
Specific: The accused broke 3 wiindows and kicked a door in.

A Good Report Is Factual

Well-written reports are also factual. There's a difference, by the way, between accurate and factual. A fact is something real that can be either proved or disproved. The fire destroyed nine homes is a statement of fact. However, further investigation may show that the fire destroyed three homes and six outbuildings. The first statement was found to be inaccurate, but it was a statement of fact versus an inference or opinion.

An inference is a conclusion based on reasoning. It becomes sound or believable if supported by facts.

Inference:

We suspected that he was driving under the influence because we could smell alcohol on his breath and because his speech was slurred.

Fact:
Blood tests confirmed he had a blood alcohol level that was twice the legal limit.

An opinion is a belief. It may or may not be appropriate to include opinions in your report. However, if you do include them, you should clearly identify them as such.

Fact:
The driver had a blood alcohol level that was twice the legal limit.

Opinion:
The driver is an alcoholic.

A Good Report Is Objective

Objective reports are fair and impartial, not influenced by emotion or opinion. One key to being objective is to avoid words whose connotations change the tone of the report.

Subjective: The man attacked an old bag lady.
Objective: The man attacked an elderly homeless woman.

An objective report includes both sides of the story and does not favor one side or another. The first account below is objective. However, the second and third are slanted to favor the wife and husband, respectively. Only the first one is appropriate.

Objective: Several witnesses reported hearing the couple arguing about money. Mr. Reilly allegedly hit his wife in the face during the argument. We found Mrs. Reilly with a bloody nose and a swollen cheek.

Slanted: Numerous witnesses reported that the couple had been fighting because Mr. Reilly couldn't hold down a job. Mr. Reilly slugged his wife in the face because he was furious that she brought up the subject. We found Mrs. Reilly with severe injuries to the face, including a bloody nose and a badly swollen cheek.

Slanted: Several witnesses reported that the couple had been arguing because Mrs. Reilly kept nagging her husband about being laid off. Mrs. Reilly became so hostile that her husband momentarily lost control and slapped her in the face. Mrs. Reilly claimed to have been badly beaten, but she had only a little bit of blood beneath her nose and a slightly red cheek.

Statements from witnesses, and other people may not be objective.

A Good Report Is Complete

A well-written report is complete. It covers the who, what, where, when, why, and how. It does not leave unanswered questions. For example, don't stop with who the victim was and who responded to the call. Include who discovered the incident, who reported it, who witnessed it, whom you talked to during your investigation, who marked and received the evidence, other people whom you notified, and so on as appropriate.

How much detail is appropriate for a given report depends largely on the incident and your department's policies. Consider, also, how the report may be used in the future. Will it be used in court someday? If so, anticipate that both the prosecution and the defense will examine the report closely. You should anticipate being questioned about every detail, including some that are not in the report. The more you put in the report, the less you have to rely on memory and the more credibility you have in the courtroom.

Remember the old adage: If it isn't documented, it didn't happen. Imagine, for example, a slip and fall where the individual suffers a spinal injury that leaves him paralyzed. When this incident goes to court, as you can predict it will, questions are raised as to whether the care rendered by first responders contributed to the paralysis. The fire captain wrote in his narrative that firefighters assessed the patient and provided basic life support, then transferred care to paramedics upon their arrival. Where in that short summary does it say that firefighters provided spinal immobilization? It may have been done, but if it isn't documented, it will become a very uncomfortable point of contention in the courtroom.

How else might the report be used someday? Will you need the information to show a trend in your city? Will you need to compare the circumstances of this incident with another one that might be related? If there are details you may need in the future, include them in the report.

Who else may read your report? Investigators? City officials? Insurance companies? Others? What information will they need? Be sure your report covers those details too.

Realize that these many of these reports are public documents and, as such, may be read by people you may not be thinking about when you write your report. For example, an author or journalist working on a book or news story might dig into public records for details about the incident or the people involved. Is there anything in your report that will later embarrass you, your agency or company?

This leads to the question of what to do with details that shouldn't be made public. For example, laws prohibit releasing confidential patient information. However, the details must be documented somewhere. So the reports need to be structured in such a way that confidential information is restricted to documents that aren't accessible to the public.

Later in this newsletter are two sections that provide additional guidelines on being complete. You can use these to trigger your thinking as you write your reports.

A Good Report Is Concise

It may seem contradictory to say that a report should be both complete and concise. However, being concise does not mean leaving out important details. Rather, it means using words economically and omitting words that do not add value. Your documents should be free of the excessive wordiness that interferes with readability.

Wordy: The engine company that arrived first on scene immediately began operations to search the first floor of the hotel and rescue anyone who might be trapped.
Concise: The first-in engine company immediately began search and rescue operations on the first floor of the hotel.

A Good Report Is Well-Organized

Poorly organized reports can leave readers feeling lost and confused, so it's important that reports be well-organized.

The best way to organize information will depend somewhat on the type of report and the complexity of the situation. A simple incident report might work best if organized in chronological order. An inspection report, on the other hand, might flow better if organized by type of violation (e.g., blocked exits in three areas) or by location (e.g., problems noted room-by-room).

A fire investigation report might require a combination approach. It may need a chronological account of what happened, then separate sections to address cause and origin analysis, evidence collected, statements from witnesses, and so forth.

A Good Report Is Clear

A clear report is one that can be easily understood and that contains no ambiguities. If different people can read the same report and come up with different interpretations, the report is not clear.

Provide specific details. As already indicated, vague references do not give readers much information. The more details you provide, the clearer the incident will be to readers. Look at the first example on the following page. What does overcrowded mean? Who says the balcony was overcrowded? The first sentence is unclear because it leaves too much open to interpretation.

Vague: The balcony collapsed because it was overcrowded.

Clear: The wooden balcony collapsed because it was overloaded.

Structural engineers confirmed that it was designed to hold a maximum of eight people. Several witnesses said there were at least fifteen people on the balcony when it collapsed.

Use diagrams, sketches, and photographs as appropriate to help illustrate the scene, and make sure the information in your report is consistent with what is depicted in your visual aids.

A Good Report Is Grammatically Correct

Many of the errors made in report writing are errors in grammar, punctuation, spelling, and word choice. Errors in grammar and punctuation can affect both the clarity and accuracy of your report. They also make you look less professional. As indicated earlier in this newsletter, this can be a source of great embarrassment in the courtroom.

It's beyond the scope of this newsletter to go into depth on how to write a grammatically correct report. However, let's look at a couple examples of common problems. Sometimes the use or omission of a comma can change the meaning of the sentence. Read the two examples below.

Essential: The second patient who was transported to Community General Hospital had third-degree burns on his hands and arms.

Nonessential: The second patient, who was transported to Community General Hospital, had third-degree burns on his hands and arms.

In the first sentence, the words printed in italics are essential to the meaning of the sentence. The first sentence refers to the second of two or more patients who were transported to Community General.

In the second sentence, the words are nonessential; they can be removed without changing the meaning of the sentence. This sentence identifies the second of two or more patients treated, not necessary the second patient sent to Community General. The first patient may be have been sent elsewhere.

Notice that the words in each sentence of the above examples are exactly the same. The only difference between the sentences is in the use or omission of commas.

The following example is something called a dangling modifier. The introductory phrase does not clearly modify the subject. It appears as if the officers, not the drunk driver, were weaving in and out of traffic.

Wrong: Weaving in and out of traffic, we suspected the man was driving under the influence.

Right: Because he was weaving in and out of traffic, we suspected the man was driving under the influence.

Use the active voice as much as possible. There are two voices in the English language: active and passive. The active voice emphasizes the one doing the action, while the passive voice emphasizes the person or thing being acted upon. The active voice is generally clearer, more powerful, more interesting, and more concise than the passive voice. Plus, as illustrated below, the whodunit is often omitted when sentences are written in the passive voice.

Active: The patient's wife was doing CPR when we arrived.

Passive: CPR was being performed prior to our arrival.

Correct spelling and word choice are also important. A typo that isn't caught by spell-checkers can change the meaning of a sentence. For example, spell-checkers won't identify if you've mistakenly identified that a patient suffers from hypotension rather than hypertension.

Other mistakes are less critical. However, when you confuse such words as its and it's or accept and except, it hurts your credibility and distracts from the content of your message.

Grammar, punctuation, and spelling may not be among your strengths, but they're vital towards writing a good report.

A Good Report Is Light on Abbreviations

Some abbreviations are acceptable in almost any document. It's certainly appropriate to use Mr., Mrs., and Dr. instead of spelling the words out. Long and cumbersome expressions are commonly abbreviated in all but the most formal writing. For example, it's acceptable to use AIDS instead of acquired immune deficiency syndrome. It's easier for both the writer and the reader. Standard abbreviations that facilitate reading are also acceptable in all but the most formal reading. Examples include psi, gpm, and mph.

Certain abbreviations may be acceptable in one application but not in others. For example, paramedics can use the abbreviation pt. for patient in patient contact reports. However, it would be inappropriate to use that abbreviation in ordinary writing. Don't abbreviate out of laziness.

Many experts recommend minimizing the use of abbreviations in ordinary writing. Using too many abbreviations or using them inappropriately can detract from your message and give readers the impression that you do not know how to write

Whodunit? Whatdunit? and So Forth

The importance of being complete was addressed earlier in the newsletter. However, the following pages contain ideas of things you may want to cover when hitting the who, what, where, when, why, and how. Obviously, the
emphasis placed on each of these questions will vary based on the type of incident and how involved it is, but these ideas can stimulate your thinking.

Who?

- Who was directly involved? (Who was injured? Who experienced the
- release?)
- Who discovered the incident? • Who reported the incident?
- Who witnessed the incident? Who saw or heard something important?
- Whom did you talk to while on scene or while investigating the incident?
- Who responded to the incident?
- Who took what actions?
- Who is the responsible party?
- Who was in possession of the property at the time of the incident? (This may be different than the responsible party.)
- Who was notified of the incident? (Did you call parents, an insurance company, or other agencies?)
- Who is the insurance carrier?
- Who collected, marked, and received evidence?
- Whom did you turn the patient or property over to?

✷ What?

- What happened? (Include type of incident and enough details to paint a picture of the incident.)
- What property was involved and to what extent?
- What was the chief complaint?
- What actions did you take?
- What were the results of your actions?
- What automatic systems were involved (alarm systems, sprinkler systems, air bags, etc.)?
- What was said?
- What evidence was found, photographed, and/or collected?
- What hazardous materials or conditions were you and your crew exposed to?
- What unusual circumstances did you encounter en route, on scene, or after leaving?
- What equipment was used?
- What equipment was damaged or contaminated? What equipment must be repaired or replaced?
- What warnings did you provide the responsible party before you left?
- What follow-up is required?

※ Where?

- Where did the incident occur? Is this the same location you were dispatched to?
- Where did the incident go if it extended beyond the point of origin?
  What exposures were impacted?
- Where were patients found? Is this the same location you were dispatched to?
- Where did the reporting party call from?
- Where was evidence found?
- Where do responsible parties and other key people live/work?
- Where did you make entry into the building?

※ When?

- When did the incident happen?
- When was the incident discovered and reported? (Delays between when the incident occurred and when it was discovered and reported can be significant.)
- When did emergency responders arrive on scene? • When did other agencies arrive?
- When was the incident brought under control? • When will follow-up activities take place?

✳ **Why?**

- Why did the incident occur? Was it accidental or intentional? What
  factors contributed to the incident?
- Why did you take the actions you did? (This is particularly important if you deviated from SOPs or if anything unusual happened.)

✳ **How?**

- How did the incident occur?
  How was the incident discovered?
- How is this incident related to other incidents (if applicable)?
- How was evidence or samples collected?
- How was information obtained?

Elements of a Complete Report

The following are other guidelines on things to include. This section includes some overlap with the previous pages. However, it also includes many items not previously addressed. The information needed for a report will vary somewhat based on the type of incident, and how the information is presented will vary depending on the forms you use in your agency. However, these pages can be used to help trigger your thinking.

Nature and Extent of Emergency (Both Actual and Reported)

Describe the nature and extent of the emergency. If there was a discrepancy between what you were dispatched to and what you found on your arrival, be sure to document that. Provide sufficient details for someone who was not there to develop a mental picture of the incident (e.g., a one-story, wood frame, single-family home with flames and smoke showing from the kitchen window on the right side of the house). Information covered in other parts of the report (e.g., the form section) does not have to be repeated in the narrative unless it makes the report clearer or easier to read.

Observations

What did you observe? Observations, like size-up, take place throughout the incident, so don't limit yourself to things observed strictly upon arrival. What did you see before your arrival (e.g., smoke showing from the station or someone seen fleeing from the scene as you approached)? Did you see anything later in the incident that might be significant?

Actions

What did you do to control the scene and mitigate the problem, and what were the results of your actions? Be specific, particularly where questions might arise later, such as in court. "Treated the patient" is not specific. Who treated the patient? What did the treatment consist of? What equipment did you use? Remember the old adage, If it isn't documented, it didn't happen.

Unusual Circumstances

Note anything out of the ordinary, particularly where evidence suggests this event may not be accidental. Did you notice signs of forced entry? Did fire protection equipment fail to function as it should? Did the fire spread in an unusual manner? Is there some connection between this incident and an earlier one you responded to? In high-profile incidents, particularly where there is loss of life or extensive losses to property or the environment, even little details can be important.

Property Damage

Describe what was damaged, as well as the type and extent of damage (e.g., heavy fire damage in the garage and heavy smoke damage throughout the house). You don't need to identify specific contents damaged unless there are unusual circumstances (e.g., it appears someone forced the safe open and removed the contents prior to the fire). However, some departments typically ask their personnel to make an estimate of dollar loss on both property and contents.

Cause

Identify the cause if possible, and provide specific observations that led to your conclusion (e.g., beading on electrical wires or paint transfer between a forklift and the cylinder it damaged). If appropriate, particularly when the cause is undetermined, identify causes that have been ruled out based on your observations (e.g., power controls in the off position or appliance unplugged). If you don't yet know the cause because the incident has been turned over to someone else for investigation, document that.

Statements Provided by Others

If you take statements from victims, witnesses, family, friends, employers, etc., document those statements, along with names and phone numbers of individuals providing those statements.

Advice, Warnings, or Information You Provided

Document any advice, warnings, or other pertinent information you provided to victims, occupants, building owners, etc. Sometimes, as is the case with EMS calls, you may have specific forms for this (e.g., the AMA—against medical advice—form). Often, however, you will need to include such warnings as part of your narrative (e.g., advised plant manager to have an electrician check the wiring before restoring power).

Disposition

How did you leave the situation? Whom did you leave the patient or property in the care of (e.g., patient was transported by AMR 314 to Community General, warehouse was turned over to the owner)? Did you refer the case to another person within your department (e.g., fire investigator) or to someone in another agency (e.g., County Health, RCMP)? If so, get a name or badge number and telephone number. What notifications did you make (e.g., utility company, building department)? Did you turn anything on or off before you left (e.g., alarm system, electricity)?

Tips for More Effective Writing

Effective writing is often critical in the hazmat arena. We rely on well written SOPs, training manuals, and other reference sources to keep us safe. Good reports can minimize our liability and build stronger court cases. Additionally, people often make judgments about our credibility and professionalism based on our writing skills.

Use the Appropriate Voice

There are two voices in the English language: active and passive. The active voice emphasizes the one doing the action. The passive voice emphasizes the person or thing being acted upon. The one doing the action may or may not even be mentioned in a sentence written in the passive voice.

Active: Firefighters decontaminated and treated seven people.
Passive: Seven people were decontaminated and treated by firefighters.

The active voice is more powerful, more interesting, and usually more concise. However, there are times when the passive voice is preferable. For example, the passive voice is useful when the one doing the action is either unknown or less important than the one being acted upon.

Active: Someone sabotaged the water treatment plant last night.
Passive: The water treatment plant was sabotaged last night.

You can also use the passive voice when you want to protect the identity of the one doing the action, such as when you want to protect a witness.

Active: Bill Petersen overheard our suspect threaten to blow up the water treatment plant.
Passive: Our suspect was overheard threatening to blow up the water treatment plant.

The passive voice is often used to sound more diplomatic, to soften the impact of a strong statement, or to avoid

Active: You must clean up this site within the next 30 days.
Passive: The site must be cleaned up within the next 30 days.

Avoid Needless Shifts

A shift is a change in structure or style midway through a sentence or paragraph. Most shifts result in confusing or awkward sentences.

Avoid shifts in number (for example, from singular to plural). Making everything plural is often easier than making everything singular. Alternately, you can rewrite the sentence to eliminate the pronoun. Notice that the last example below is clearer and more concise than any of the others.

Inconsistent:
If a person mixes drinking and driving, they may end up in jail.

Revised:
If a person mixes drinking and driving, he or she may end up in jail.

Revised:
If people mix drinking and driving, they may end up in jail.

Better:
People who mix drinking and driving may end up in jail.

Avoid shifts in person (for example, from third person to second person). Put everything in the same person or rewrite the sentence entirely.

Inconsistent:
If a person stops breathing, you can suffer permanent brain damage in four to six minutes.

Revised:
If you stop breathing, you can suffer permanent brain damage in four to six minutes.

Revised:
If a person stops breathing, he or she can suffer permanent brain damage in four to six minutes.

Revised:
People who stop breathing can suffer permanent brain damage in four to six minutes.

Avoid inappropriate shifts in voice (for example, from active to passive). Sometimes a shift in voice is appropriate because it keeps the reader focused on a single subject. The following example shifts from an active voice to a passive voice, but the subject, fire, does not change.

The fire burned out of control for hours, but was extinguished by early morning.

If a shift in voice also involves a shift in subject (for example, from we to the children), the resulting sentence will be awkward and confusing. The following sentence was corrected by putting everything in the active voice.

Inconsistent: As we pulled up to the burning structure, the children inside could be heard screaming desperately for help.

Revised: As we pulled up to the burning structure, we could hear the children inside screaming desperately for help.

Avoid shifts in discourse (for example, from an indirect question to a direct question).

Inconsistent: I asked whether the product is flammable and, if so, is it within its flammable range.

Revised: I asked whether the product is flammable and, if so, whether it is within its flammable range.

Revised: Is the product flammable and, if so, is it within its flammable range?

Avoid shifts in point of view. Point of view refers to the person through whose eyes the story is told. The first example below begins with an observation made by rescue workers, then abruptly switches to the driver's point of view. The problem was corrected by writing everything in the eyes of the rescue workers.

Inconsistent: We found the vehicle resting on its roof at the bottom of the embankment. The driver struggled to crawl out throughthe broken window, afraid the leaking gasoline would ignite.

Revised: We found the vehicle resting on its roof at the bottom of the embankment. We could see the driver struggling to crawl out through the broken window, apparently afraid that the leaking gasoline would ignite.

Use Parallel Structure

To use parallel structure means to use like form or structure in your writing. In other words, when two or more items or ideas are presented in the same sen-tence or list, the wording should be similar.

Use parallel structure when two or more items are combined with words such as and, but, or, nor, or yet.

Nonparallel: Playing with matches can lead to fires and getting burned.

Parallel: Playing with matches can lead to fires and burn injuries.

Use parallel structure when presenting lists. Notice below how switching from identifying in the first sentence to identify in the second makes all the verbs parallel.

Nonparallel: Our objectives are to;

1. Ensure our personal safety.
2. Isolate the area
3. Identifying the hazardous material.

Parallel: Our objectives are to;

1. Ensure our personal safety.
2. Isolate the area.
3. identify the hazardous material. Use parallel structure with elements being compared or contrasted.

Nonparallel: Roger decided to become a police officer rather than a career in the fire service.

Parallel: Roger decided to become a police officer rather than a firefighter.

Parallel: Roger decided on a career in law enforcement rather than in the fire service.

Avoid Mixed Sentences

Avoid mixed constructions — sentences with two or more incompatible grammatical structures.

Mixed: By doubling your distance from a radioactive source reduces your risk of exposure by 75%.

Revised: Doubling your distance from a radioactive source reduces your risk of exposure by 75%.

Revised: By doubling your distance from a radioactive source, you reduce your risk of exposure by 75%.

Make logical connections — subjects and predicates that make sense together. The example below is subtle. However, deciding to close the highway is not really the problem. You can decide all you want to, but nothing happens until you act. Thus, it's really the act of closing the highway, not the decision to do so, that caused the problems.

Mixed: Deciding to close the highway caused problems for commuters all evening.

Revised: Closing the highway caused problems for commuters all evening.

Avoid Sentence Fragments

Avoid sentence fragments. A sentence fragment is a part of a sentence that is incorrectly punctuated as if it were a complete sentence.

Ensure your sentence has both a subject and a verb.

Fragment: Arrived on scene at 1357 hours.
Revised: We arrived on scene at 1357 hours.

Fragment: Her eye irritated. She complaining about pain.
Revised: Her was eye irritated. She was complaining about pain.

Pull fragmented phrases and clauses into nearby sentences, . . .

Fragment: We finally figured out who the bomber was. Thanks to a tip from an anonymous caller.

Revised: We finally figured out who the bomber was, thanks to a tip from an anonymous caller.

Or create two independent sentences.

Revised:

We finally figured out who the bomber was.
We credit a tip from an anonymous caller.

Avoid Run-Ons and Comma Splices

Avoid run-on sentences — two independent clauses joined without any punctuation whatsoever.

Run-on: The smoke was thick they had trouble advancing.

Avoid comma splices — two independent clauses joined by a comma alone, rather than by a comma and a coordinating conjunction (e.g., and, but, or, so).

Comma Splice: The smoke was thick, they had trouble advancing. Either punctuate properly, . . .

Revised: The smoke was thick. They had trouble advancing.

Revised: The smoke was thick, so they had trouble advancing. Use a semicolon and transitional expression, . . .

Revised: The smoke was thick; as a result, they had trouble advancing.

Or make one clause subordinate to the other.

Revised: The smoke was thick, making it difficult for them to advance.

Revised: They had trouble advancing because the smoke was thick.

Avoid Misplaced, Squinting, and Dangling Modifiers

A modifier is a word, phrase, or clause that qualifies or limits the meaning of another word or group of words. Modifiers include adjectives and adverbs, as well as words, phrases, and clauses that serve as adjectives and adverbs.

Readers generally associate modifiers with the nearest words they might logically modify. When modifiers are put in the wrong place, it can result in confusing, amusing, or embarrassing sentences. The following is an example of what is called a misplaced modifier. The first sentence implies the fire department does more damage than the fire. This is not the message we want to give the public.

Misplaced: The fire was extinguished before any appreciable damage was done by the fire department.

Revised: The fire was extinguished by the fire department before any appreciable damage was done.

When a modifier falls between two words or phrases and can conceivably modify the words or phrases on either side, it is said to be "squinting." Squinting modifiers create ambiguity.

Squinting: People who drink and drive frequently cause accidents.

When you say a sentence aloud, you can use pauses and vocal inflection to make your meaning clear: People who drink and drive—pause—frequently cause accidents. However, someone reading the same sentence cannot hear your pauses and vocal inflection and may interpret the sentence differently: People who drink and drive frequently—pause—cause accidents. Even if readers eventually interpret the sentence correctly, if they had to read it two or three times to do so you've done them a disservice. You can avoid this confusion by repositioning the modifier.

Clear: Frequently, people who drink and drive cause accidents.

Do not try to fix a squinting modifier by inserting a comma to make your readers pause. While every comma signals a pause, not every pause warrants a comma. It would be grammatically incorrect to insert a comma between the words drive and frequently in the example on the previous page.

A dangling modifier is one that does not clearly describe anything in the sentence. Although the connection may be clear in the writer's mind, it is not necessarily clear in the reader's. Dangling modifiers often result in very awkward sentences. The first example below implies that the chief (not the build-ing) was totally engulfed in flames when he made his decision.

Dangling: Totally engulfed in flames, the chief decided to let the build-ing burn and protect the exposures instead.
Revised: Since the building was totally engulfed in flames, the chief decided to let it burn and protect the exposures instead.

Here's another example. The first sentence below suggests that the subject of the sentence, you, might be ruled inadmissible in court. It says nothing about the evidence.

Dangling: To be ruled admissible in court, you must ensure the chain of custody is unbroken.
Revised: To be ruled admissible in court, evidence must be maintained with an unbroken chain of custody.
Revised: For evidence to be ruled admissible in court, you must ensure the chain of custody is unbroken.

Be Concise

Avoid careless and unnecessary repetition.

Repetitious: The smoke-filled attic was charged with smoke.

Revised: The attic was charged with smoke.

The key to eliminating unnecessary repetition is being able to identify words that can be omitted without changing the meaning of the sentence. Consider the following examples.

Repetitious	**Concise**
red in color	red
circular in shape	circular
dangerous in nature	dangerous

Don't fill your sentences with empty words. Many phrases can be replaced by one or two words.

If It Doesn't Look Good, It Isn't Worth Reading!

While it may be an exaggeration to say that if something doesn't look good, it isn't worth reading, it's true that the nicer a document looks, the better the chance that someone will read it. If your message is important enough to put in writing, it's worth making the document look good.

People do not often go out of their way to read something unless they have to read it or want to read it. If your document looks professional, attractive, and user-friendly, people are more inclined to want to read it.

Remember, too, that you are often competing with many other demands for your readers' time and attention. You can't afford to turn readers off with documents that look ugly, uninviting, or difficult to read.

When you make an effort to make your documents look nice, it communicates to readers that your care about them and their needs, that you take pride in your work, and that what you have put in writing is important to you.

Choosing Be Choosing Between Serif and Sans Serif Type tween Serif and Sans Serif Type

Type is grouped into two basic styles: serif and sans serif. Serifs are lines or curves projecting from the end of a letter (as illustrated below). Serif typefaces have those lines or curves; sans serif faces do not. Serifs help guide the reader's eye from one letter to the next. So serif type is considered better for prolonged reading, such as body text in a training manual.

Sans serif faces, on the other hand, are generally thought to be easier to read at very large sizes or very small sizes. They work well for headlines where the type is larger than the rest of the text. They also work well for forms where the type is small and the space is limited.

4BOT 4FSJG

Using multiple typefaces (e.g., serif for body text and sans serif for headlines) is acceptable if done wisely. However, using too many typefaces can give the appearance of a ransom note pasted together. Careless intermingling of regular, bold, and italic type can have the same effect. The type becomes a distraction, taking attention away from the message. The page looks messy and amateurish, not clean and professional.

Aligning Text

There are four basic options for aligning text.

Justified text (flush on both margins) generally gives documents a neater, more professional appearance. However, because the normal space between letters and words is altered to justify the text, justification sometimes results in uneven spacing.

Flush left (ragged right) text is relatively easy to
read and allows even word spacing. It can also reduce
the excessive hyphenation sometimes found in justified text.

Flush right (ragged left) is difficult to read because the reader has more
trouble finding the beginning of each line. It can be used for special
effects, captions, or short sidebar comments. Excessive use of flush right
is not recommended, however.

Centered text works well for most headlines and for formal invitations
or announcements. It does not work well for body text because it's
difficult to read for the same reason that flush right text is.

Using FULL CAPS

> *Use FULL CAPS sparingly ... if you must use them at all.*

When we read, we recognize not only the words themselves but also the shapes of the words. Words set in upper and lower case have distinctive and recognizable shapes. The monotonous rectangular shapes of words set in full caps lack these visual clues, making documents written in full caps harder to read.

Avoid thinking that readers will perceive the message as being more important if the words are set in full caps. Readers are more likely to subconsciously dismiss the text as too difficult to read and therefore not worth the effort.

More effective ways to emphasize important text include using bold or italic type, increasing the font size, repeating important words in headlines or pull quotes, and using graphics to draw attention to the message. What works best will vary from one application to another.

Adding Emphasize with Type

Emphasis can be added by varying the type as long as the document is easy to read and pleasant to look at.

Boldface type is generally the most effective way to make something pop out on the page. Yet too much bold type can undermine the intended effect and make the page look dark and intimidating. In addition, if print quality is poor, the type has a tendency to plug up, making the words difficult to read.

Italic type provides a subtle contrast to the main text. It is used primarily when subtlety, as opposed to strength, is desired. Since italic type is more difficult to read than plain text, it should be used sparingly.

<u>Underlining</u> is the least desirable because it is hard to read. Readers have difficulty separating the words from the lines beneath them. Some letters are especially difficult for readers to identify because they run into the underlining:

<u>g, j, p, q, y.</u>

Using Boxes and Backgrounds

Enclosing type in a box is another way to draw attention to important information. Use a line width that will complement your type rather than compete with it. And very important—leave a border of white space between the text and the lines of your box. Text that touches the lines is hard to read and ugly to look at.

> Leave a border of white
> space between your text   and the lines of your box.

> Text that touches the lines is
> Hard to read and ugly to look at

When using text against a gray, colored, or patterned background, maintain enough contrast to ensure the type is easy to read. Consider using larger or darker type so that it stands out against the background. If the background is dark, you may need to reverse the text instead. However, studies have shown the black text on a white background is as much as 40% easier to read than white text on a black background.

Using Headlines and Subheads

Headlines and subheads are organizational tools to help readers identify what information is being presented in the text that follows. Subheads help break the information into manageable segments and allow readers to quickly locate specific information. They also add visual interest to the page by breaking up large expanses of text. This makes reading less of a chore, which increases the effectiveness of your message.

Headlines and subheads should be set off from the main text by using larger type, bolder type, or both. They may be set in a different typeface for greater contrast. They may be aligned differently from the body text. For example, a headline or subhead might be centered while the rest of the text is justified.

People may subconsciously skip over headlines and subheads when they read, so it's important to ensure that the text that follows clearly communicates the message without requiring readers to stop and backtrack.

Using Illustrations and Photographs

Illustrations and photographs can emphasize important information and help readers understand difficult concepts. They can also enhance the appearance of a document, making it easier and more enjoyable to read.

Have a purpose for every image. Avoid meaningless "designer droppings" that are distracting to the reader. Avoid overshadowing the message with graphic elements that steal the reader's attention away from the text.

Use high quality images that complement the text and that complement one another. Bad or inappropriate artwork or photos detract from the message and reflect poorly on the writer.

Crop, reduce, or enlarge photographs as needed to make them clearer or more dynamic. Consider editing out distracting information to help your audience focus on key elements. Use captions to explain or supplement images as needed.

Don't infringe on copyrights when using images created by other people.

Get permission.

Finding the Right Words
distinguishing between similar words with slightly different meanings

It is sometimes difficult to choose the right words when similar words have different meanings. This is the first in a series of newsletters designed to help you distinguish between two or more similar words.

accept or except

Accept is a verb meaning "to receive or to agree to." Except is usually a preposition or a conjunction (both connecting words) meaning "but or excluding."

The chief accepted all of our suggestions except the one to implement a driver's training program for the volunteers.

Except can also be used as a verb meaning "to exclude or leave out."

Earthquake damage is excepted from coverage in the basic insurance policy.

advice or advise

Advice is a noun that refers to a recommendation or suggestion. Advise is a verb meaning "to give counsel, to recommend, or to suggest."

When people ask us for advice as to how to make their homes more secure, we advise them to install deadbolt locks.

affect or effect

Affect is usually a verb meaning "to influence or change." Effect is usually a noun referring to a result or a state of being operational.

Smoke inhalation can affect a person's judgment.

The effects of smoke inhalation can be seen after only a brief exposure.
Effect is sometimes used as a verb meaning "to produce a result."

We must effect a quick rescue.
Affect is used as a noun only in the field of psychiatry. It refers to an expressed or observed emotional response.
The affect is typical of a schizophrenic individual.

assure, ensure, or insure

Assure, ensure, and insure all mean "to make secure or certain." However, there are subtle differences between them. Assure refers to persons, with the sense of setting a person's mind at rest. Ensure means to "make sure" or "make safe." Insure is used when referring to insurance.

We must ensure there are no hot spots before we can assure the residents that the fire is completely extinguished.

I hope they were insured against fire.

cite, sight, or site

Cite can mean "to order someone to appear in court," "to give an example or quote an authority," or "to recognize someone, such as for outstanding service."
I am citing you for exceeding the speed limit.

The instructor cited directly from the penal code.

Bill was cited for his many contributions to the fire service. Sight can be used as either a verb or a noun referring to vision.

Mary lost her sight after her optic nerves were damaged by scarlet fever. Site refers to a position, location, place, or scene.
Police found her body at an isolated site along the river.

device or devise

Device is a noun referring to a thing, an invention, or a contrivance. Devise is a verb meaning "to contrive, plan, or invent."

I want to devise a device to help us quickly locate victims in a smoke-filled room.

elicit or illicit

Elicit means "to evoke or bring out." Illicit means "illegal or unlawful."

See if you can elicit information from any of our snitches regarding the sale of illicit drugs in the neighborhood.

incite or insight

Incite means "to stir up or prompt." Insight refers to an intuitive understanding.

If they incite a riot, we are going to need more help.
Give me some insight on what we can expect tonight.

miner or minor

A miner is someone who works in a mine.

Rescuers worked feverishly to save three miners trapped underground after a methane gas explosion rocked through the coal mine.

As a noun, minor can refer to person under legal age or to an academic course of study that is subordinate to a major. As an adjective, minor means "not serious" or "lesser in importance."
He was arrested for having sex with a minor.

Catherine sustained only minor cuts and bruises.

personal or personnel

Personal means "individual or private." Personnel refers to employees.

We have issued personal alarm devices to all personnel.
Personals (usually plural) refers to a column or section of a newspaper or magazine that contains personal notices or items.
The murderer is selecting his victims from among women who advertise in the personals.

principal or principle

The noun principal can refer to the person in charge of an organization (often an educational one), the primary person responsible for something (such as the principal [versus the accessory] in a crime), or to a capital sum of money (as distinguished from interest or profit).

The principal is concerned about students bringing weapons to school.

These boys are accessories to the crime. We still haven't identified the principal.

The interest rates are so high that I'm hardly making a dent in the principal.

Principal is also used as an adjective meaning "primary or most important."

My principal complaint is that we didn't get enough hands-on training in the class.

Principle refers to a fundamental rule, a code of conduct, or a natural tendency.

We operate under the principle that a person is considered innocent until proven guilty in a court of law.

It is against my principles to provide a certificate of completion to someone who cannot perform proficiently.

It is a principle of nature that gases expand when they are heated.

steal or steel

Steal means "to take illegally or without permission" or "to move quietly or secretively." It is also used informally in reference to a bargain.

He tried to steal my purse.

The surveillance tape shows the burglar stealing about through the electronics store late at night.

Steel is a form of iron metal.

Steel beams, girders, and columns will fail relatively quickly in a fire if not protected by gypsum, concrete, or an appropriate spray-on application. Steel is also used as a verb meaning "to fill with determination or resolve."

Steel yourself. It's not a pretty scene.

to, too, or two

To is a preposition. To is also used in conjunction with a verb to form an infinitive (for example, to drink). Too is an adverb meaning "also," "excessively," or "very." Two is the number 2.

Monica had too much to drink. She should have gone to bed. She went for a drive instead and ended up injuring two people when she lost control of her car.

weather or whether

The noun weatherr efers to wind, rain, snow, and other atmospheric conditions. The verb weather means "to endure and come safely through something."

Bad weather contributed to the accident.

If we pull together, I know we can weather this crisis. Whether is a conjunction used to introduce or imply alternatives. Whether the ambulance goes Code 2 or Code 3 to the hospital depends largely on the patient's condition.

It is sometimes necessary to use the expression whether or not for clarity. However, if whether alone will suffice, drop the words or not.
Whether or not he is lying, I don't trust him. I can't tell whether he is lying.

Test Your Knowledge

In each of the sentences below, circle the word that is most correct.

1. There have been to/too/two many accidents to dismiss this latest event as a coincidence.

2. The drug affects/effects the central nervous system.

3. Police anticipate that she will return to the cite/sight/site of the crime to destroy any evidence.

4. My first priority is to assure/ensure/insure the safety of my crew.

5. Everyone accept/except the bus driver had only miner/minor injuries.

6. My advice/advise is to train all personal/personnel in how to use the fire extinguishers.

7. Police found an explosive device/devise in the lobby.

8. I couldn't tell weather/whether he was transporting elicit/illicit drugs.

9. The principal/principle hazard with this chemical is toxicity.

10. The detectives have more incite/insight as to what's happening.
Check Your Answers

The following are answers to the quiz on the previous page.

1. There have been <u>too</u> many accidents to dismiss this latest event as a coincidence.

2. The drug <u>affects</u> the central nervous system.

3. Police anticipate that she will return to the <u>site</u> of the crime to destroy any evidence.

4. My first priority is to <u>ensure</u> the safety of my crew.

5. Everyone <u>except</u> the bus driver had only <u>minor</u> injuries.

6. My <u>advice</u> is to train all <u>personnel</u> in how to use the fire extinguishers.

7. Police found an explosive <u>device</u> in the lobby.

8. I couldn't tell <u>whether</u> he was transporting <u>illicit</u> drugs.

9. The <u>principal</u> hazard with this chemical is toxicity.

10. The detectives have more <u>insight</u> as to what's happening.

Finding the Right Words
distinguishing between similar words with slightly different meanings

It is sometimes difficult to choose the right words when similar words have different meanings. This is the second in a series of newsletters designed to help you distinguish between two or more similar words.

bad or badly

Bad is an adjective meaning "not good." Badly is an adverb meaning "in a defective, incorrect, or undesirable way."

John was hurt badly in a bad accident.

Most experts say that you should use bad as an adjective either before a noun (bad decision, bad mistake) or after a linking verb (feel bad, look bad). Although many people use the phrase feel badly, it is best to avoid it in writing.

I feel bad (not badly) about what happened to him.

bring or take

Bring refers to moving something closer to the speaker. Take refers to moving something away from the speaker.

Please bring me the stretcher. Then you can help me take the patient out to the ambulance.

can or could / may or might

Can and could indicate ability or power. May and might are used to express permission. Can and may are often used interchangeably in conversation when asking or granting permission. However, in writing, you should maintain the distinction between the two.
I don't know if we can pull together a mass casualty drill that quickly. (ability)

May I check your injury? (permission)

May and might also indicate possibility.

Do you think the tank might rupture? (possibility)

Can/could and may/might are often used interchangeably when referring to possibility. Many experts insist you should maintain a distinction between the words, but there are times when any of them may be appropriate. The tank can rupture means it has the ability to do so. The tank may rupture means that it has the ability to do so and that there is a likelihood of the rupture occurring.

dragged or drug

Drug is a nonstandard form of dragged, the past tense and past participle of drag. Use dragged, not drug.

We dragged the victim out of the burning building.

good or well

Good is an adjective used to modify a noun or pronoun. Well is an adverb used to modify a verb, an adjective, or another adverb.

We have a good crew that works well together.

When referring to the state of one's health, it is possible to use either good or well. To feel or look well means "to be in good health," whereas to feel good generally means "to be in good spirits." To look good means "to look pleasing in appearance."

hanged or hung

Both hanged and hung are used to describe "death by hanging." Hanged is the preferred form when referring to a legal execution, while hung is more common when referring to suicide. Hung is also used for all meanings other than "death by hanging."

Wilson was hanged by the neck for his crimes. Three days later, his former cellmate hung himself.

Elizabeth hung her head in shame.

lay or lie

The verbs lay and lie are often confused because they are so similar. However, lay means "to put or place" someone or something, whereas lie means "to rest or recline." Lay is a transitive verb; it requires a direct object to complete its meaning. Lie is an intransitive verb; it never takes a direct object.

In other words, you can lay something, but you cannot lie anything.

I ordered him to lay the gun down and come out with his hands up. Please lie.

Lie also means "to remain in a position of inactivity or concealment."

They were lying in ambush for us.
It is easy to confuse the various forms of lie and lay, especially since the past tense form of lie is lay.

Present	Past	Present Participle	Past Participle
lay [place]	laid [placed]	laying [placing]	(had) laid [placed]
lie [rest]	lay [rested]	lying [resting]	(had) lain [rested]

To lie, meaning "to speak falsely," is unlikely to be confused with lay. The past tense and past participle is lied. The present participle is lying.

leave or let

Leave means "to depart or to go away from." It can also mean "to allow to remain in the same place or condition." Let means "to allow or permit."

If you leave the scene of an accident without stopping, you can be charged with felony hit-and-run.

The doctor suggested that I leave the bandage in place for at least 48 hours.

Don't let him get away.

Leave and let can be used interchangeably when followed by a noun or pronoun and the word alone. However, use let alone, not leave alone, in the sense of "not to mention."

Leave/let me alone.

I don't like missing out on any fires in our jurisdiction, let alone (not leave alone) one of this magnitude.

raise or rise

The verbs raise and rise are often confused because they are so similar. However, raise is a transitive verb; it requires a direct object to complete its meaning. Rise is an intransitive verb; it does not take a direct object. In other words, you can raise something, but you cannot rise anything.
I don't like to raise the 24-foot ladder by myself when it is this windy. Our aerial ladder rises to a height of 100 feet.

Raise and rise are also used as nouns. Raise is used primarily to indicate an increase in wages. Rise is more versatile and is used in connection with most other increases.still while I check for injuries.

Our contract calls for a 10% raise over the next two years.

A sudden rise in temperature may cause organic peroxides to become highly unstable.

The following are the different forms of the verbs raise and rise.

Present	Past	Present Participle	Past Participle
raise	raised	raising	(has) raised
rise	rose	rising	(has) risen

real or really

Real is an adjective used to modify a noun or pronoun. Really is an adverb used to modify a verb, an adjective, or another adverb.

Those look like real injuries.

You do a really good job of applying moulage.

Real is often used informally as an adverb: You do a real good job. However, you should avoid using real as an adverb in writing.

set or sit

The verbs set and sit are often confused because they are so similar. Set is primarily a transitive verb, requiring a direct object to complete its meaning.
Use set when your meaning is "to put or place" something. Sit is chiefly an intransitive verb, not requiring a direct object. Use sit when you mean "to be seated."

Set the gun down on the table, then we'll sit down and talk.

Both set and sit have numerous other meanings. Set is relatively easy. For example, one sets goals, sets things on fire, or sets traps. Sit, however, is used in other situations where one might mistakenly use set.

Use sit when you mean "to cause to be seated," "to remain quiet or inactive," or "to be accepted as indicated."

If I could only sit him down and talk to him, I could probably figure out what he's up to.

Let's sit on this for a while before we make a decision. The defendant's story doesn't sit well with me.

The following are the different forms of the verbs set and sit.

Present	Past	Present Participle	Past Participle
set	set	setting	(has) set
sit	sat	sitting	(has) sat

sure or surely

Sure is an adjective used to modify a noun or pronoun. Surely is an adverb used to modify a verb, an adjective, or another adverb.
I was sure Rick was innocent. Rick was surely innocent.

Sure is often used informally as an adverb: He sure seemed innocent to me. However, you should avoid using sure as an adverb in writing.

Test Your Knowledge

In each of the sentences below, circle the word that is most correct.

1. Steven feels bad/badly about causing the fire.

2. I don't feel good/well. I need to lay/lie down.

3. The situation was real/really dangerous.

4. Please let me know when I can/may take a day off.

5. The victim committed suicide. She hanged/hung herself in the garage.

6. I asked Truck 5 to raise/rise the aerial on the A side of the building.

7. I'm going to set/sit this one out.

8. Engine 7 laid/lay 400 feet of five-inch hose.

9. Please bring/take the coffee to the command post.

10. Who do you think could/might have started the fire?

Check Your Answers

The following are answers to the quiz on the previous page.
1. Steven feels <u>bad</u> about causing the fire.

2. I don't feel <u>good/well</u>. (Use well if you mean "in good health" or good if you mean "in good spirits.") I need to <u>lie</u> down.

3. The situation was <u>really</u> dangerous.

4. Please let me know when I <u>may</u> take a day off. (While either can or may is
acceptable in informal speech, may is preferable in writing.)
5. The victim committed suicide. She <u>hung</u> herself in the garage.
6. I asked Truck 5 to <u>raise</u> the aerial on the A side of the building.
7. I'm going to <u>sit</u> this one out.
8. Engine 7 <u>laid</u> 400 feet of five-inch hose.

9. Please <u>bring/take</u> the coffee to the command post. (Use bring if you are at the command post, requesting coffee be brought to you. Use take if you are elsewhere, asking someone to take the coffee away from you and to the command post.)

10. Who do you think <u>could/might</u> have started the fire? (Both words are often used interchangeably when referring to possibility. Technically, however,
could suggests ability, whereas might implies possibility. The correct choice in this example would depend on your meaning.)

Finding the Right Words
distinguishing between similar words with slightly different meanings

It is sometimes difficult to choose the right words when similar words have different meanings. This is the third in a series of newslettersdesigned to help you distinguish between two or more similar words.

almost or most

Almost is an adverb meaning "nearly." Most is an adjective meaning "the great-
est quantity." Do not use most to mean almost in formal writing. The first example below is faulty because only an adverb (almost) can be used to modify an adjective (all).

Wrong: Most all of my money was stolen.

Right: Almost all of my money was stolen.
Right: Most of my money was stolen.

amid, among, amongst, or between

Use amid when referring to something that cannot be counted. We found the body amid (not among) the debris.
In general, use between when referring to two items and among when referring to three or more. (Amongst is chiefly a British expression. Use among instead.)

The responsibilities were divided among each person on the task force. Most of the responsibility was divided between Jan and Bill.
Use between rather than among to show a relationship involving three or more persons or things when the items, considered individually rather thancollectively, are linked to the others.

A lot of tension exists between the various gangs in our city.

Between fighting fires, writing books, and trying to run a business, I don't have much free time.

Between also means "in a space separating two points, objects, time periods,
etc."
The patient's condition deteriorated between the time we arrived on scene and the time we were able to extricate her from the vehicle.

amount or number

Use amount when referring to the sum total of things in bulk or to a mass that cannot be counted. Use number when referring to the sum total of things that can be counted.
We can't determine the number of victims still in the building because there is a large amount of debris blocking our access.

as or because

The word as may be used to mean "because," "since," "when," or "while." Therefore, you should not use as if the meaning may be vague or ambiguous.

Unclear: Diners started to panic as they noticed smoke coming from the kitchen.
Clear: Diners started to panic because they noticed smoke coming from the kitchen.
Clear: Diners started to panic when they noticed smoke coming from the kitchen.

because or since

The word since can be used to mean either "because" or "from then until now." Therefore, its meaning can sometimes be ambiguous. If you mean because in sentences such as these, use it. That will eliminate the ambiguity.

Brice is limping because he injured his knee.

beside or besides

Beside and besides are both prepositions. Beside means "next to." Besides means "in addition to" or "except."
The maid found the gun beside the victim. She said she didn't see or hear anything unusual besides the gunshot.
Besides is also an adverb meaning "furthermore, moreover, or also."
Besides, there is nothing we can do for him now.

bi- or semi- (annual, monthly, weekly)

The prefix bi- can mean either "twice each" or "every two." Therefore, biannual,
bimonthly, and biweekly can all cause confusion for readers. It is better to use the prefix semi- (for example, semiannual) when you mean "twice." However, twice each" or "every two" is ultimately less confusing than any prefix.

complement or compliment

Both complement and compliment can be used either as nouns or as verbs. Complement refers to completing something. Compliment refers to praise, com-mendation, or admiration.
The white gloves complement the Class A uniform nicely. The chief complimented the crew on a job well done.

continual or continuous

Continual means "occurring regularly and repeatedly." Continuous means "constantly, without interruption."

We've had a continual stream of requests for sandbags.

Continuous rain over three days contributed to heavy flooding in the area.

fewer or less

Fewer refers to a smaller number. Less refers toa smaller degree or a smaller amount.

We need fewer police officers than do comparable cities our size because we have less crime.

Some experts say that fewer should be used for plural nouns (fewer accidents, fewer crimes) and that less should be used for singular mass nouns (less smoke, less money) and singular abstract nouns (less crime, less violence). However, less than is used (rather than fewer than) when referring to plural nouns ex-pressed as a unitary measure (less than 20 minutes, less than $1000 dollars, less than 50 feet, less than 80 pounds).

imply or infer

Imply means "to suggest." Infer means "to assume or conclude."

Shari implied that she had been sexually molested by her father when she was a baby.

We inferred from her comments that Shari's mother had known about the molestation, but did nothing to stop it.

incidence or incidents

Incidence refers to rate of occurrence. Incidents refers to individual events.

The high incidence of cancer may be linked to a hazardous materials incident we responded to in 1980.

liable or likely

Liable means "legally responsible" or "in danger of." Likely means "probably." Liable and likely are often used interchangeably when referring to probability. However, some experts insist that liable should be used in reference only to undesirable consequences.

You are likely to need help lifting the patient and liable to hurt yourself if you don't get some help.

ordinance or ordnance

An ordinance is a law, rule, or regulation. Ordnance refers to military weapons and ammunition.

Can we adopt an ordinance against transporting military ordnance through the city?

percent or percentage

Percent and percentage both refer to a rate or proportion per hundred. However, percent is used in conjunction with a number. Percentage is used with adjectives such as large and small, not with specific numbers.

Alcohol is a factor in a large percentage (over 60 percent) of all fatal automobile accidents.

practicable or practical

Practicable means "feasible or capable of being put into practice." Practical means "useful or sensible." Practicable can be applied to objects, plans, and so forth, but not to people. Practical can be applied to both people (a practical person) and things.
It may not be practicable to evacuate everyone in the threat area. It may be more practical to direct everyone to shelter in place until the vapor cloud disperses.

Note: Just because something is practicable (feasible) doesn't mean that it is practical (sensible).

precede or proceed

Precede means "to go before." Proceed means "to move or go forward."
John preceded me into the room.
We'll proceed on your signal.

toward or towards

Both toward and towards are acceptable, though toward is more common. Whichever one you choose, use it consistently.

Test Your Knowledge

In each of the sentences below, circle the word that is most correct.

1. The earthquake displaced a large amount/number of people.

2. There were fewer/less arrests for drunk driving this year than last.

3. "Your entire complement/compliment is en route," the dispatcher advised.

4. We found almost/most all of the victims before nightfall.

5. I didn't mean to imply/infer that I thought you started the fire on purpose.

6. The military ordinance/ordnance is stored at the south end of the complex.

7. Only a small percent/percentage of our firefighters have been trained to the hazmat technician level.

8. We've had several similar incidence/incidents lately.

9. Are you taking any other medications beside/besides nitroglycerin?

10. The suspected preceded/proceeded to run in the opposite direction.

Check Your Answers

The following are answers to the quiz on the previous page.

1. The earthquake displaced a large <u>number</u> of people.

2. There were <u>fewer</u> arrests for drunk driving this year than last.

3. "Your entire <u>complement</u> is en route," the dispatcher advised.

4. We found <u>almost</u> all of the victims before nightfall.

5. I didn't mean to <u>imply</u> that I thought you started the fire on purpose.

6. The military <u>ordnance</u> is stored at the south end of the complex.

7. Only a small <u>percentage</u> of our firefighters have been trained to the hazmat technician level.

8. We've had several similar <u>incidents</u> lately.

9. Are you taking any other medications <u>besides</u> nitroglycerin?

10. The suspected <u>proceeded</u> to run in the opposite direction.

Finding the Right Words
distinguishing between similar expressions with different meanings

It is sometimes difficult to choose the right words when similar expressions have different meanings. This is the fourth in a series of newsletters designed to help you distinguish between two or more similar words or expressions.

account for or account to

You can account for either someone or something. To account for someone means "to have an accounting of." To account for something means "to give an explanation or to answer for one's actions."

We've accounted for everyone who was known to be in the building at the time of the blast.

Can you account for your whereabouts on the night of the murder? To account to someone means "to answer to or respond to a person."
You will have to account to your probation officer for your whereabouts last night.

agree on, agree to, agree upon, or agree with

To agree on or agree upon means "to reach an understanding." Agree to means "to accept a plan or proposal." Agree with means "to concur with" a person or an idea.

I don't agree with your assessment of the situation, but I will agree to investigate further if we can agree on how to best proceed.

compare to or compare with

Compare to means "to show a likeness or resemblance."

People often compare the color of Sunnyvale's yellow fire engines to that of a school bus.

Compare with is used to show actual comparisons (similarities and differences).

We'll have to compare the prints we found at the scene with those of our suspect.

Many experts say that only compare with should be used to show comparisons.
Others say that either compare to or compare with may be used for this purpose.

correspond to or correspond with

Correspond to means "to match or be in agreement with." Correspond with means "to exchange letters."

The information on the MSDS does not correspond to the information we received from CHEMTREC.

I have corresponded with firefighters all over the country.

could care less or could not care less

Do not use could care less when you mean "do not care at all." The correct expression is could not care less.

The vandals couldn't care less about what it costs to repair the damage.

decide on or decide to

Use decide on before a noun or noun phrase. Use decide to before a verb.

We had to decide on a plan of action. We decided to use a defensive attack.

differ from or differ with

Differ from means "to be unlike." Differ with means "to disagree."
Mark's symptoms differ from those of the other patients.
I differ with you on the diagnosis of his illness.

different from or different than

Different from is preferred in most applications.

This counterfeit bill is different from most of the others we have seen.

Different than is considered acceptable when different from would result in a wordy or awkward sentence.

Awkward: I would have managed the incident in a different way from the way in which you managed it.

Revised: I would have managed the incident in a different way than you did.

emigrate (from) or immigrate (to)

Emigrate means "to leave a country," whereas immigrate means "to come to another country."
They emigrated from Europe.
They immigrated to the United States.

fail in or fail to

Use fail in before a noun or noun phrase. Use fail to before a verb.

We failed in our attempt to convince the jury, although I fail to understand why.

practice for, practice of, or practice to

Use practice for or practice to when practice is a verb. Use practice of when practice is a noun.

Will you help me practice for the physical ability test?

The practice of recapping needles greatly increases the risk of exposure to disease.

reconcile to or reconcile with

Reconcile to means "to accept a condition." Reconcile with means "to settle a quarrel or dispute."
It wasn't until Sam was able to reconcile with his father that he was able to reconcile himself to the loss of his son.

speak to or speak with'

Speak to means "to tell something to someone." Speak with means "to discuss."

We intend to speak to your parents about your reckless behavior.

The mayor wants to speak with the chief about yesterday's explosion at the plastics company.

sympathy for or sympathy with

Sympathy for means "compassion for." Sympathy with refers to sharing another's
feelings.

We need to show sympathy for those people whose homes were damaged or destroyed.

Even though I am in sympathy with your position, I don't have the budget to hire more police officers.

wait for, wait on, or wait out

Wait for means "to remain ready for someone or something." Wait on means "to serve." Wait out means "to remain inactive during the course of something."

Let's wait for backup before we go in.

We were dispatched to a domestic dispute call before the waitress could wait on us.

They had to wait out the blizzard before they could continue the search.
Test Your Knowledge

In each of the sentences below, circle the expression that is most correct.

1. The two-in/two-out rule requires us to wait for/wait on backup.

2. He showed no sympathy for/sympathy with his victims.

3. The new standard is significantly different from/different than the old one.

4. I could care less/couldn't care less about the dangers.

5. Let's compare the evidence to/with evidence collected at the last three fires.

6. Can you account for/account to the unusual burn patterns?

7. Do you agree to/agree with her decision?

8. The patient's responses don't correspond to/correspond with what we see on the monitor.

9. The M.O. differs from/differs with that of his previous crimes.

10. Our personnel are having a hard time reconciling themselves to/with our first line-of-duty death in more than two decades.

Check Your Answers

The following are answers to the quiz on the previous page.

1. The two-in/two-out rule requires us to <u>wait for</u> backup.

2. He showed no <u>sympathy for</u> his victims.

3. The new standard is significantly <u>different from</u> the old one. (Different from is generally preferred over different than, although either may be used.)

4. I <u>couldn't care less</u> about the dangers.

5. Let's <u>compare</u> the evidence <u>with</u> evidence collected at the last three fires.

6. Can you <u>account for</u> the unusual burn patterns?

7. Do you <u>agree with</u> her decision?

8. The patient's responses don't <u>correspond to</u> what we see on the monitor.

9. The M.O. <u>differs from</u> that of his previous crimes.

10. Our personnel are having a hard time <u>reconciling</u> themselves <u>to</u> our first

Incident Report Form

Protecting Yourself

Today if you are running a business then you might be aware that insurance claims are on the rise employee is really very difficult. Employees required to complete reports for your company should be reliable and dedicated. The employees should be dependable on which you can trust. There are some industries out there where incidents occur frequently and people may get injured.

In such situation most staff get confused in finding the best possible way to document the incident that occurred in the work place. The best possible thing that you can do in such situation is to record the details in an *incident* report form.

```
                    INCIDENT REPORT
Business _____    Date_____
Address _____    City _____ State _____
Complainant
_____
Last Name            First Name            Initial
_____
Address       City             State        Zip
_____
Home Telephone             Business Telephone
Type of Incident
_____
Theft      Accident      Property Damage      Other
Injury
First aid given?        Yes_____    No_____
First aid refused?      Yes_____    No_____
EMS called?             Yes_____    No_____
```

When you as an employer hire employees for your company then illness, injury, conflict and other incidents occur in the workplace and are the part of your responsibility that you need to assume.

As we all know that human beings are social creatures and companies should have all the possible ways to record and keep the details of the incidents occurred on their premises. If the company has the records and details of the incident occurred on their premises then it will not only help to decrease the level of blameworthiness that is often placed on occupiers but also it will help to find out the main cause of the incident. In this way you can rectify the problem and document the incident for future reference.

In an **incident report form** you have some areas that you need to fill out such as position, name and the name of the authorized parties involved in the incident. Apart from this in the form you also need to mention all the details about the incident like name of the supervisors or managers that respond to the incident, what type of injuries the person had, the main cause of the incident, how the incident occurred exactly etc.

If you stay organized then it will not only help you to prevent incidents from happening at your workplace but will also help you to manage the situation in a collected and calm manner.

There is some very advanced and acceptable software now days that will guide staff through the reporting process and print the end result for filing and distribution.

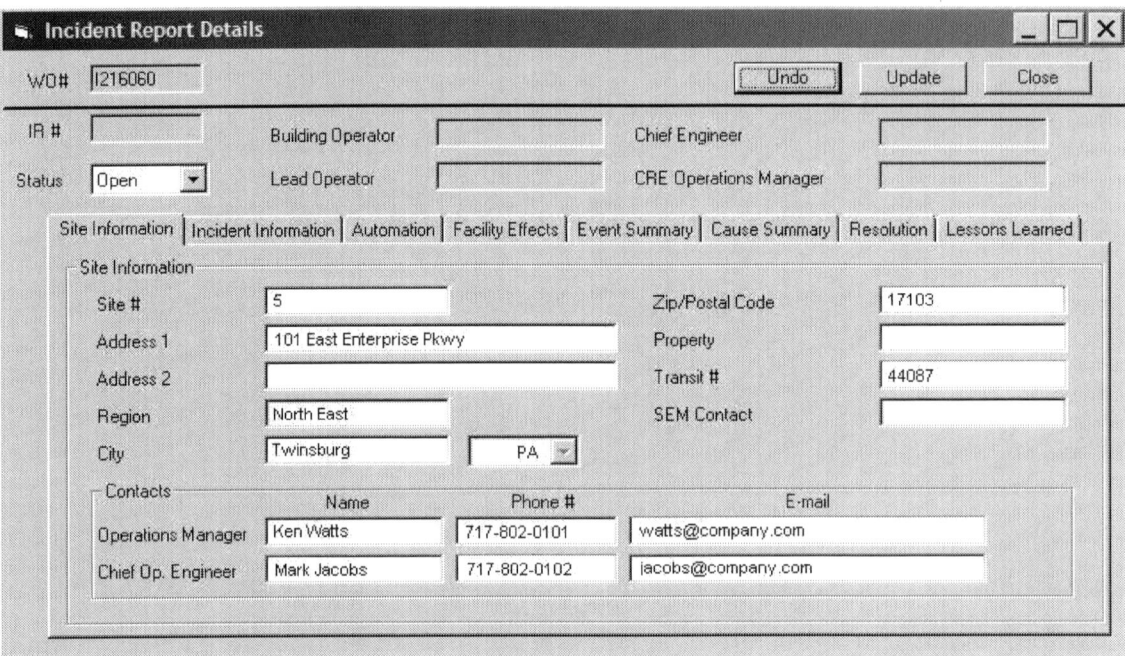

http://www.reportexec.com

http://www.iviewsystems.com

http://www.customerexpressions.com

THIS TRAINING MANUAL SHOULD BE USED ONLY AS A GUIDE.

RPM Publishing, Toronto Canada.
Copyright © 2012
All rights reserved. Published 2012
Printed in Canada

No part of this book can be reproduced or transmitted in any form or by any means,
Electronic or mechanical, including photocopying, recording, or by any information
Storage and retrieval system, without permission in writing from the Publisher and Author.

www.riskprotectionmanagement.com

REPORT WRITING FOR SECURITY GUARDS
www.riskprotectionmanagement.com

ALTERED AND COUNTERFEIT IDENTIFICATION
Bar and Nightclub Edition

A must have for Bar and Nightclub Security and Bartenders
No More Guessing On How To Check ID
What To Look For
How To Be Sure
What To Do

Jam Packed with detection tricks and tips whats out there, whats on the net and How to protect yourself.

CERTIFICATE COURSE - FULL CERTIFICATION AVAILABLE

CLUB DRUGS AND NARCOTICS
Just Released !!

What You and Your Staff Need To Know To Prevent Charges
What Are The Current Drug Trends In Clubs
How Are They Sneaking It In
Can Somebody Set Up Shop In Your Club ?

Drug Detection Screeniong and Search Tips

AVOID THOSE COSTLY DRUG OFFENCE CHARGES

CERTIFICATE COURSE - FULL CERTIFICATION AVAILABLE

SECURITY GUARD TRAINING MANUAL
PROVINCE OF ONTARIO EDITION

Get Ready For Provincial Testing of Security Guards
This Course has over 390 Pages of Secunty Training Information
Everything You Will Need To Know !

ITS ALL HERE INCLUDING A SPECIAL
Alcohol and Gaming Commission Section

ON SITE TRAINING AVAILABLE FOR LARGE GROUPS

CERTIFICATE COURSE - FULL CERTIFICATION AVAILABLE

REPORT WRITING FOR SECURITY GUARDS   www.riskprotectionmanagement.com

INCIDENT REPORT BOOK
Includes Incident Reports and Use Of Force Report

Don't Drop The Information Ball
When The Police or A Statement of Claim Arrive Have All
The Information You Need To protect Yourself In Court
Document It At The Time - Don't Be Trying To Remember
Months or Years Later

Use of Force Report Required By Law - August 2009

DOCUMENT THE INCIDENTS AND PROTECT YOURSELF

FIRE SAFETY PLAN
A Complete Guide To Your Premises Plan

You Have To Have One - It's The Law !
Fire Protection Services Charge Thousands of Dollars For It
Follow Our Fill In The Blanks Version and Save The Money
Fill It In Send It To Us - We'll Complete It Bind It
And Have it Ready For Fire Department Approval

Don't Take The Risk - If The worst Happens You Could Be Liable

KIT CONTAINS ALL NECESSARY FORMS AND DOCUMENTS

DRIVERS LICENSE IDENTIFICATION
Canada or North America Versions

Permit Minor on Premises - Serve Alcohol To A Minor
Full Color Illustrations of All Legal Drivers Licenses and Identification
Read The Hidden Codes - Know The Hidden Graphics
Don't Get Caught By A Fake ID

Use of Fake ID is on the Rise - Teens Are Getting Into Clubs

FULL COLOR ILLUSTRATIONS AND SAMPLES

Printed in Great Britain
by Amazon.co.uk, Ltd.,
Marston Gate.